YOU DON'T HAVE
TO BE CRAZY
TO WORK HERE . . .

BUT IT SURE HELPS

YOU DON'T HAVE TO BE CRAZY TO WORK HERE . . .

BUT IT SURE HELPS

and Other Office Hang-Ups

by
WAYNE B. NORRIS

PRICE/STERN/SLOAN
Publishers, Inc., Los Angeles
1986

Portions of this book originally appeared under the title
The Big Book of Photocopier Humor.

Copyright © 1984, 1986 by Wayne B. Norris
Illustrations copyright © 1986 by Wayne B. Norris and Price/Stern/Sloan Publishers, Inc.
Published by Price/Stern/Sloan Publishers, Inc.
410 North La Cienega Boulevard, Los Angeles, California

ISBN: 0-8431-1496-7

DEDICATION

This book is dedicated to my dearest brother, Brett Harold Norris, who was killed by a drunk driver when he was twenty-eight years old. A portion of my proceeds from this book will go toward furthering the work of such organizations as Mothers Against Drunk Driving (M.A.D.D.) in the hopes that tragedies of this type may soon be relegated to history.

The cartoon "Watch your language" is in commemoration of the short time I spent in the offshore oil industry. It is dedicated to all my friends from that business, living and dead, and especially to mentors Jim Parker, Jerry Clauser, Bob Christianson and Tom Bachurin. Most of all, it is dedicated to the late Ramsay Parks, who would certainly qualify as one of the greatest deep-sea divers of all time.

ACKNOWLEDGEMENTS

I was fortunate to have assembled the talents of many creative people in this endeavor. I am deeply indebted to the following individuals:

Joe Doyle, Susanne Chess, Joe Boucher, Barbara Ryan, Nancy Fredericks, John Iwerks, Linda Horowitz, Karen Karsh, Alan Clark, Gerry Ichikawa, Joan Roche, David Spence, Bambi Williams, Martha Cody, Joe Herring, Dan Poynter, L. Spencer Humphrey and, of course, my wife Maryann and my son Brian and our respective families for all their love.

INTRODUCTION

Of the several characteristics that seem to distinguish Humans from members of other mammalian species, one of the most interesting is the need people have to stick stuff up on walls. Or bulletin boards. Chimpanzees do not post things on sides of their arboreal nests. Raccoons show zero interest in this odd activity. Even the Lemming, the one animal with whom Humans have the most in common, shows no tendency to communicate by tacking, stapling or taping stuff to vertical surfaces.

Humans, however, discovered this compulsion in themselves 25,000 years ago when they began drawing bison on the sides of their caves in Altamira, Spain. Later, the Delphic Oracle invented graffiti by having this zinger chiseled over her door — "He who knows not and knows that he knows not is truly wise." The Roman Legions plastered their barracks with signs saying "SPQR" (the Senate and the People of Rome) which led, in only one and a quarter millenia, to "Kilroy Was Here."

And so on, until today, when due to the proliferation of the Photo Copier, public pasting and thumb tacking has become a major art form. (A major art form is one that anyone can do, as opposed to minor art forms, which are practiced by folks with limited abilities such as Rembrandt van Rijn, Picasso, Degas, Daumier, et al.)

This handy Slab Size Book is filled with stickupable stuff. It contains jokes, aphorisms, philosophical admonitions, rude remarks and much that is highly educational. Everything here is meant to be copied and put up on some wall or bulletin board. Or ceiling if you are a very tall person. If you have no Copier, you can, of course, simply rip pages out of this book and carry on. But remember: *He who knows not and knows not that he knows not. . . HE is the one we're trying to sell this book to.*

ROGER PRICE

TAKE HEART!

THE ONLY PERSON WHO EVER GOT
ALL HIS WORK DONE BY FRIDAY WAS...

ROBINSON CRUSOE

YOU WANT IT WHEN ??!

WARNING!
THESE PREMISES ARE GUARDED
BY AN
ATTACK RECEPTIONIST!

 **NOTICE:**

BE SURE BRAIN IS IN GEAR
BEFORE ENGAGING MOUTH

ORGANIZATIONAL CHARTS

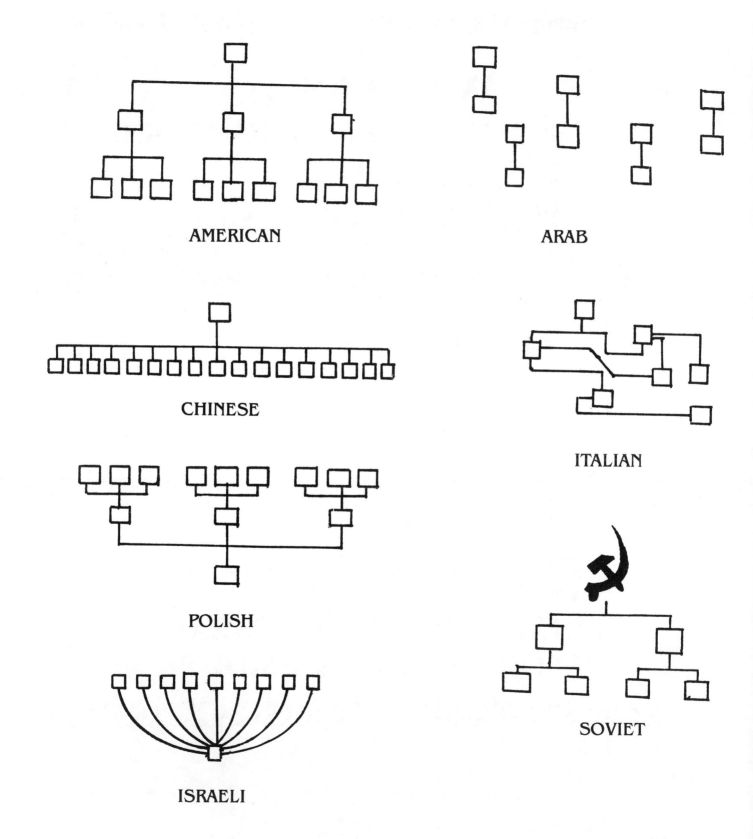

AMERICAN

ARAB

CHINESE

ITALIAN

POLISH

SOVIET

ISRAELI

THE DIFFERENCE BETWEEN HEAVEN AND HELL:

In heaven,
    the English are the Cops
    the French are the Cooks
    the Germans are the Mechanics
    the Italians are the Lovers
    the Russians are the Poets
    the Americans are the Inventors
    the South Africans supply the Raw Materials
    the Tahitians take care of the Human Rights,
    and . . . it's all organized by the Swiss.

In hell,

    the English are the Cooks
    the French are the Mechanics
    the Germans are the Cops
    the Swiss are the Lovers
    the Russians are the Inventors
    the Americans are the Poets
    the South Africans take care of the Human Rights
    the Tahitians supply the Raw Materials,
    and . . . it's all organized by the Italians.

**GETTING ANYTHING DONE AROUND HERE
IS A LOT LIKE MATING ELEPHANTS...**

- **IT INVOLVES A LOT OF
  SCREAMING AND ROARING;**

- **IT HAPPENS AT A HIGH LEVEL;**

- **AND IT TAKES ALMOST 2 YEARS
  TO SEE THE RESULTS!**

IT'S BEEN MONDAY ALL WEEK.

BEAM ME UP SCOTTY.

Dear _____,

How's it ☐ going? ☐ coming? ☐ been? Are you enjoying
life ☐ more? ☐ less? ☐ more or less?

Personally, I've been feeling ☐ up. ☐ down. ☐ hung over. It takes
a little getting used to being ☐ without you. ☐ being with someone
else. ☐ being gay.

These past few weeks, I've been getting
into ☐ trouble. ☐ bestiality. ☐ the theory of relativity. It's done
wonders for my ☐ acne. ☐ impotence. ☐ plants. You should try it.

I'm thinking of going back to ☐ mommy. ☐ nature. ☐ school. It
would probably improve my ☐ disposition. ☐ finances. ☐ sex life.
And then again, maybe not.

I still miss all those ☐ moments together. ☐ nights
together. ☐ nasty insults. I think what I miss most about you is
your ☐ smile. ☐ body. ☐ tattoo.   It always seems to remind me of
my ☐ mother. ☐ father. ☐ parole officer.

Wishing you ☐ the best. ☐ the worst. ☐ were here.

P.S. When you get the chance, would you please return
my ☐ clothes? ☐ money? ☐ teddy bear?

STICKS AND STONES MAY BREAK MY BONES

BUT WHIPS AND CHAINS EXCITE ME!

INTERNATIONAL HOUSE
of PANIC

Believe it or not insurance claims.

Coming home, I drove into the wrong house and collided with a tree I don't have.

The other car collided with mine without giving warning of its intentions.

I thought my window was down but found out it was up when I put my hand through it.

I collided with a stationary truck coming the other way.

A truck backed through my windshield into my wife's face.

A pedestrian hit me and went under my car.

The guy was all over the road. I had to swerve a number of times before I hit him.

I pulled away from the side of the road, glanced at my mother-in-law, and headed over the embankment.

In my attempt to kill a fly, I drove into a telephone pole.

I had been shopping for plants all day and was on my way home. As I reached an intersection a hedge sprang up obscuring my vision. I did not see the other car.

I had been driving my car for forty years when I fell asleep at the wheel and had an accident.

I was on my way to the doctor's with rear end trouble when my universal joint gave way causing me to have an accident.

As I approached the intersection, a stop sign suddenly appeared in a place where no stop sign had ever appeared before. I was unable to stop in time to avoid the accident.

To avoid hitting the bumper of the car in front, I struck the pedestrian.

My car was legally parked as it backed into the other vehicle.

An invisible car came out of nowhere, struck my vehicle, and vanished.

I told the police I was not injured; but on removing my hat, I found that I had a skull fracture.

I was sure that the old fellow would never make it to the other side of the roadway when I struck him.

The pedestrian had no idea what direction to go, so I ran over him.

I saw the slow moving, sad faced old gentleman as he bounced off my car.

The indirect cause of this accident was a little guy in a small car with a big mouth.

I was thrown from my car as it left the road. I was later found in a ditch by some cows.

The telephone pole was approaching fast. I was attempting to swerve out of its path when it struck my front end.

I was unable to stop in time and my car crashed into the other vehicle. The driver and passengers then left immediately for a vacation with injuries.

THANK YOU
FOR NOT LAUGHING AT THIS CAR

WELCOME TO CALIFORNIA . . .

NOW GO HOME

November 15, 1950
Export Coffee Company
134 West 29th Street
New York, New York
U.S.A.

Schentlemans:

Die letzte two packages von koffee ve got from you vas mitt ratt schidt gemischt. Der koffee may be goot enuf, but die ratt durds schbeil der trade. Ve dit not zee die ratt durds in der semples you sendt down to us.

So mich time it takes to pick der ratt durds out from der kaffee, yah! Ve order der klean kaffee undt you schipt schidt mixt mit der kaffee. It vos a mistake, yah? Ve like you to schipp us der kaffee in vun sack und der ratt schidt in vun udder sack, und den ve mix it opp to soot der costomer. Pleaze ride iff ve schouldt schipp back der schidt und keep der kaffee; or keep der schidt und schipp back der kaffee; or schipp back der hol schitten verks.

Ve vant to do rite in dis madder, but ve do not like dis dam ratt schidt bizness.

Mitt much respekt

Hans Gruber

HG/ts

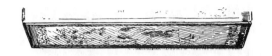

WHEN ALL ELSE FAILS, READ THE DIRECTIONS

IT IS BETTER TO REMAIN SILENT, AND RISK THE CHANCE OF APPEARING IGNORANT, THAN TO SPEAK, AND REMOVE ALL DOUBT.

ARIES   TAURUS   GEMINI   CANCER   LEO   VIRGO

ARIES - MARCH 21 to APRIL 19

You are the pioneer type and hold most people in contempt. You are quick-tempered, impatient, and scornful of advice. You are not very nice.

_____, Francois "Papa Doc" Duvalier, and "Boss" Tweed are Aries people.

TAURUS - APRIL 20 to MAY 20

You are practical and persistent. You have a dogged determination, and work like hell. Most people think you are stubborn and bullheaded. You are very likely either a Communist or a Fascist.

_____, Adolph Hitler, Pol Pot, Ayatollah Ruhollah Khomeini, and Rudolf Hess are Taurus people.

GEMINI - MAY 21 - JUNE 20

You are a quick thinker and intelligent. People like you because you are bisexual. However, you are inclined to expect too much for too little. This means you are cheap. Geminis are known for committing larceny.

_____, Martin Bormann, Yuri Andropov, and the Marquis de Sade are Gemini people.

CANCER - JUNE 21 to JULY 22

You are sympathetic and understanding of other people's problems. They think you are a sucker. You are always putting things off. That's why you'll never make anything of yourself. Most welfare recipients are Cancers.

_____, Vidkun Quisling, and John Dillinger are Cancer people.

LEO - JULY 23 to AUGUST 22

You consider yourself a born leader. Others think you are pushy. Most Leo people are bullies. You are vain, and dislike criticism. Your arrogance is disgusting. Leo people are often thieves.

_____, and Benito Mussolini are Leo people.

VIRGO - AUGUST 23 to SEPTEMBER 22

You are the logical type, and hate disorder. This nit-picking is sickening to your friends. You are cold and unemotional, and sometimes fall asleep while making love.

_____ and Jesse James are Virgo people.

LIBRA   SCORPIO   SAGITTARIUS   CAPRICORN   AQUARIUS   PISCES

LIBRA - SEPTEMBER 23 to OCTOBER 22

You are the artistic type, and have a difficult time with reality. If you are a man, you are more than likely gay. Chances for monetary gain are excellent. Libra women make good prostitutes.

_____ and Heinrich Himmler are Libra people.

SCORPIO - OCTOBER 23 to NOVEMBER 21

You're shrewd in business, and cannot be trusted. You will achieve the pinnacle of success because of your total lack of ethics. Many Scorpio people are murdered.

_____, Joseph Goebbels, and Lee Harvey Oswald are Scorpio people.

SAGITTARIUS - NOVEMBER 22 to DECEMBER 21

You are optimistic and enthusiastic. You have a reckless tendency to rely on guts, since you lack talent of any kind. The majority of Sagittarians are drunks or dope fiends. People laugh at you a great deal.

_____, Billy the Kid, Joseph Stalin, and Anastasio Somoza are Sagittarians.

CAPRICORN - DECEMBER 22 to JANUARY 19

You are conservative, and afraid of taking risks. You don't do much of anything, and are lazy. There have been few Capricorns of any lasting importance. Capricorns should avoid standing in one place too long, as they tend to take root.

_____, Herman Goehring, and Al Capone are Capricorns.

AQUARIUS - JANUARY 20 to FEBRUARY 18

You have an inventive mind and are inclined to be progressive. You lie a great deal. On the other hand, you are inclined to be careless and impractical, and you make the same mistakes over and over again. People think you are stupid.

_____ and Benedict Arnold are Aquarius people.

PISCES - FEBRUARY 19 to MARCH 20

You have a vivid imagination and often think you are being followed by the FBI or the KGB. You have minor influence over your associates, and people resent your flaunting of your power. You lack confidence, and are generally a coward. Pisces people do terrible things to small animals.

_____, Emperor Bokassa, and Adolf Eichmann are Pisces people.

NOTICE
OFFICE OF
CIVILIAN DEFENSE
WASHINGTON, D.C.

INSTRUCTION   TO   PERSONS   ON PREMISES
IN CASE OF NUCLEAR BOMB ATTACK

UPON THE FIRST WARNING:

1. STAY CLEAR OF ALL WINDOWS.
2. KEEP HANDS FREE OF GLASSES, BOTTLES, CIGARETTES, ETC.
3. STAND AWAY FROM CHAIRS, LOOSE EQUIPMENT, AND FURNITURE WITH SHARP OR BREAKABLE PARTS.
4. LOOSEN NECKTIE; UNBUTTON COAT AND ANY OTHER RESTRICTIVE CLOTHING.
5. REMOVE GLASSES; EMPTY POCKETS OF ALL SHARP OBJECTS SUCH AS PENS, PENCIL, ETC.
6. TAKE COVER UNDER A TABLE OR OTHER STURDY OBJECT.
7. IMMEDIATELY UPON SEEING THE BRILLIANT FLASH OF NUCLEAR EXPLOSION, BEND OVER AND PLACE YOUR HEAD FIRMLY BETWEEN YOUR LEGS.
8. **THEN KISS YOUR ASS GOODBYE.**

Dear Uncle Sam, Please send money...

Excerpts from letters to local welfare offices.

I am forwarding my marriage certificate and six children. I have seven, but one died which was baptized on a half sheet of paper.

I am writing the welfare department to say that my baby born 2 old. When do I get my money?

Mrs. Jones has not had any clothes for a year and has been visited regularly by the clergy.

I cannot get sick pay. I have six children. Can you tell me why?

I am glad to report that my husband who is missing is dead.

This is my 8th child. What are you going to do about it?

Please find out for certain if my husband is dead. The man I am now living with can't eat or do anything till he knows.

I am very much annoyed to find you have branded my son illiterate. This is a dirty lie as I was married a week before he was born.

In answer to your letter, I have given birth to a boy weighing ten pounds. I hope this is satisfactory.

I am forwarding my marriage certificate and 3 children, one of which is a mistake as you can see.

My husband got his project cut off 2 weeks ago and I haven't had any relief since.

Unless I get my husband's money pretty soon, I will be forced to live an immoral life.

You have changed my little boy to a girl. Will this make any difference?

I have no children as yet as my husband is a truck driver and works day and night.

In accordance with your instructions I have given birth to twins in the enclosed envelope.

I want my money as quick as I can get it. I've been in bed with the doctor for two weeks and he doesn't do me any good. If things don't improve I will have to send for another doctor.

NEW AGE EDUCATION CENTER
Fully Accredited Extension Courses

PHILOSOPHY DEPARTMENT

V1100   Creative Suffering
V1101   Overcoming Peace of Mind
V1102   You and Your Birthmark
V1103   Guilt Without Sex
V1104   The Primal Shrug
V1105   Ego Gratification Through Violence
V1106   Molding Your Child's Behavior Through Guilt and Fear
V1107   Whine Your Way to Alienation
V1108   Dealing with Post-Realization Depression
V1109   How to Overcome Self-Doubt Through Pretense and Ostentation

BUSINESS DEPARTMENT

BB-1   "I Made $100 in Real Estate"
BB-2   Money Can Make You Rich
BB-3   Packaging and Selling Your Child
BB-4   Career Opportunities in El Salvador
BB-5   How to Profit from Your Own Body
BB-7   The Underachievers Guide to Very Small Business Opportunities
BB-8   Tax Shelters for the Indigent
BB-9   Looter's Guide to America's Cities

ARTS AND CRAFTS DEPARTMENT

DM101   Self-Actualization Through Macrame

DM102   Needlecraft for Junkies
DM103   Cuticle Crafts
DM104   Gifts for the Senile
DM105   Bonsai Your Pet
DM106   How to Draw Genitalia

MOTOR SKILLS DEPARTMENT

EF404   Sinus Drainage at Home
EF408   Basic Kitchen Taxidermy
EF409   1001 Other Uses for Your Vacuum Cleaner
EF410   The Maintenance and Repair of Your Virginity
EF412   How to Convert a Wheelchair into a Dune Buggy
EF416   Christianity and the Art of RV Maintenance

HEALTH DEPARTMENT

L202   Creative Tooth Decay
L204   Exorcism and Acne
L206   The Joys of Hypochondria
L208   High Fiber Sex
L210   Suicide and Your Health
L212   Biofeedback, and How to Stop It
L214   Skate Yourself to Regularity
R406   Understanding Nudity
R408   Tapdance Your Way to Social Ridicule
R410   Optional Body Functions

Limited Enrollment, so send form now with your registration check. Form must be filled out completely in order to process your course enrollment. Group rates are available on request. Details of courses and dates of meetings will be mailed to you upon acceptance of enrollment.

ENROLLMENT FORM

NAME _____ JOB TITLE _____

ADDRESS _____ PHONE NUMBER _____

COURSE NUMBERS _____

 # DEFENSE WORKERS

JOIN THE
MOTHER'S MARCH
FOR A

BIGGER DEFENSE BUDGET

**Left-handed people are
the only ones
in their right minds.**

Roses are red,
     Violets are blue,
I'm schizophrenic,
     And so am I.

A WRITER'S BIGGEST PROBLEM IS THAT WHEN HE STARES OUT THE WINDOW, EVERYONE THINKS HE'S NOT WORKING.

A WRITER'S BIGGEST PROBLEM IS THAT WHEN SHE STARES OUT THE WINDOW, EVERYONE THINKS SHE'S NOT WORKING.

THE LAW OF FIXED LOCATION:

NO MATTER WHERE YOU GO,

THERE YOU ARE!

DON'T BE AFRAID TO ASK DUMB QUESTIONS.
THEY'RE A LOT EASIER TO HANDLE THAN DUMB MISTAKES.

...WHATEVER IT IS,
IT'S DEAD!

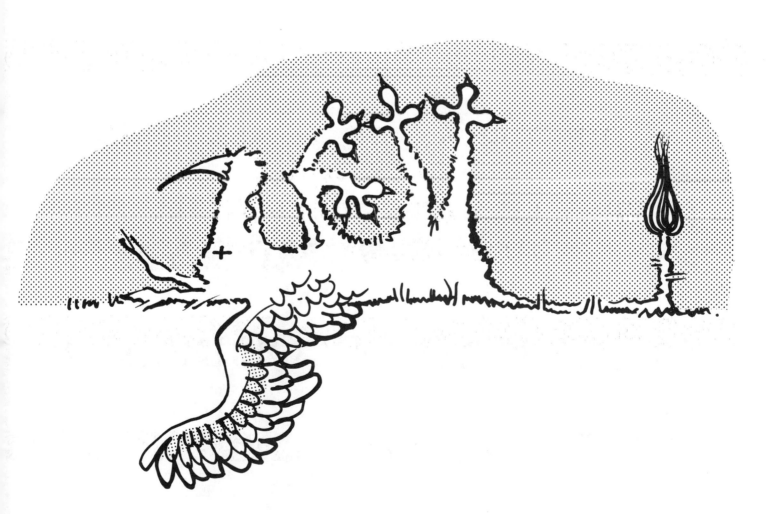

Garbage In...
Gospel Out!

OH, THE AGONY OF DELETE!

EXECUTIVE'S
MANAGEMENTSPEAK
ACCESSORY KIT

... A CAN OF WORMS

... TURMOIL

...A ROLL OF RED TAPE

... A BOX OF ROUND TUIT'S (FOR PEOPLE WHO CAN'T GET AROUND TO IT)

... PANDORA'S BOX

...A SPOON (FOR "FEEDBACK" FROM EMPLOYEES)

... BAKING SODA (FOR AVOIDING "HEARTBURN")

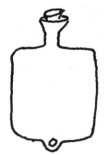

...AND A HOT WATER BOTTLE (TO GIVE A "WARM FEELING" ABOUT PROJECTS)

IF YOU CAN'T DAZZLE 'EM WITH YOUR
BRILLIANCE,
**BAFFLE 'EM WITH YOUR
B.S.!**

**IF YOU CAN'T WIN,
MAKE THE ONE AHEAD OF YOU
BREAK A RECORD**

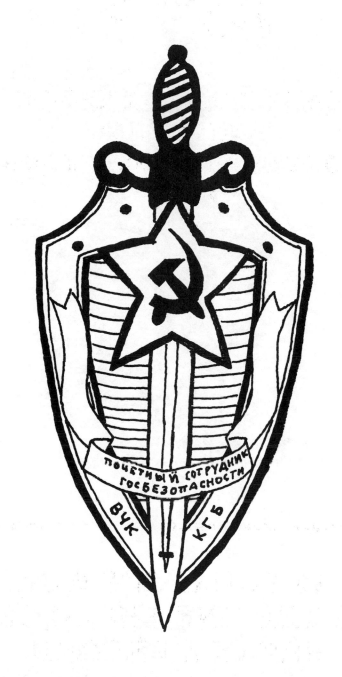

The Official Emblem of the KGB

PEOPLE WHO LOVE SAUSAGE

AND RESPECT THE LAW

SHOULD NEVER WATCH EITHER

OF THEM BEING MADE.

IT ISN'T PRETTY BEING EASY

NORRIS' LAW:

**Almost nothing is impossible
if you really put the screws to the right people.**

NEVER TRY TO TEACH A PIG TO SING;
IT WASTES YOUR TIME,
AND IT ANNOYS THE PIG.

JUST BECAUSE YOU'RE NOT PARANOID...
DOESN'T MEAN THEY'RE NOT OUT TO GET YOU!

HELP!
THE PARANOIDS ARE AFTER ME!

WARNING

THIS MACHINE IS SUBJECT TO BREAK-DOWNS DURING PERIODS OF CRITICAL NEED

A special circuit in the machine, called a "critical detector," senses the operator's emotional state in terms of how desperate he or she is to use the machine. The critical detector then creates a malfunction proportional to the desperation of the operator. Threatening the machine with violence only aggravates the situation. Likewise, attempts to use another machine may cause it to malfunction also. (They belong to the same union.) Keep cool, and say nice things to the machine. Nothing else seems to work.

HAVE YOU HUGGED YOUR PORCUPINE
TODAY?

CONGRATULATIONS ON YOUR
TREMENDOUS FEAT!

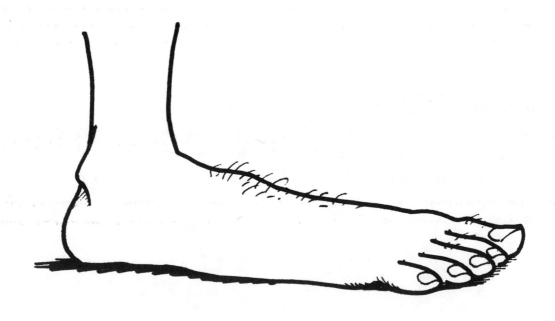

THE GOLDEN RULE:
HE WHO HAS THE GOLD
MAKES THE RULES

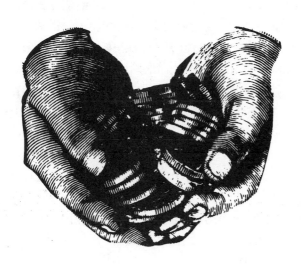

I DON'T SMOKE . . .
KISS ME, AND TASTE THE DIFFERENCE!

THE BAROMETER

The story is told of a physicist who, upon transferring from one university to another during the course of his advanced studies, was required by some stroke of fate to repeat a freshman physics course, taught by a professor many years his junior. Highly contemptuous of this rather arbitrary ruling, he sat for his first mid-term exam, and was faced with the problem, "How do you determine the height of a building by using a barometer?" In a fit of indignation, he wrote as an answer, "Go up to the top of the building, drop the barometer over the side, time it until it hits the ground, and use the equation for falling bodies."

The professor came to him after class, sensing his indignation, and said, "Come now! Can't you think of another way?" He assumed this would act as a broad hint.

Instead, the physicist replied, "Certainly! You could measure the height of the barometer, and the length of its shadow, and then compute the height of the building from the length of ITS shadow, using the law of similar triangles.

"Or, you could tie the barometer to a length of string, making a pendulum. Then, you could time the period of the pendulum at the bottom and the top of the building, and compare the periods, getting the height from the equation for the gravitational gradient.

"But the superior method by far would be to go to the building superintendent's office, tap on the door with the barometer, and when someone comes to answer, simply say, 'I will give you this fine barometer if you will just tell me how high this building is!' "

AROUND HERE, WE DO <u>PRECISION</u> GUESSWORK!

I THINK WE'RE ALL BOSONS ON THIS BUS

I SAW THAT PUNCH COMING,

SO I BLOCKED IT WITH MY CHIN!

KEEP YOUR FRIENDS CLOSE . . .
BUT KEEP YOUR ENEMIES CLOSER.

THE KING HAS NO CLOTHES!

HOW YOU CAN TELL WHEN IT'S GOING TO BE A ROTTEN DAY

You wake up face down on the pavement.

You put your bra on backwards, and it fits better.

You call Suicide Prevention, and they put you on hold.

You see a "60 Minutes" news team waiting in your office.

Your birthday cake collapses from the weight of the candles.

Your son tells you he wishes Anita Bryant would mind her own business.

You want to put on the clothes you wore home from the party, and there aren't any.

You turn on the news, and they're showing emergency routes out of the city.

Your twin sister forgot your birthday.

You wake up and discover your waterbed broke, and then realize that you don't have a waterbed.

Your car horn goes off accidentally and remains stuck as you follow a group of Hell's Angels on the freeway.

Your wife wakes up feeling amorous, and YOU have a headache.

Your boss tells you not to bother to take off your coat.

The bird singing outside your window is a buzzard.

You wake up and your braces are locked together.

You walk to work and find your dress is stuck in the back of your pantyhose.

You call your answering service, and they tell you it's none of your business.

Your blind date turns out to be your ex-wife.

Your income tax check bounces.

You put both contact lenses in the same eye.

Your pet rock snaps at you.

Your wife says, "Good morning, Bill" and your name is George.

MILLIONAIRES ARE A DIME A DOZEN!

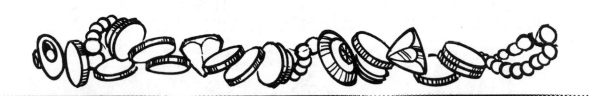

BETTER DEAD THAN MELLOW!

IN 1950, THE CHEAPEST COMPUTERS COST
THE SAME AS THE MOST EXPENSIVE ROLLS
ROYCE. IF BOTH HAD DEVELOPED AT THE
SAME RATE, BY 1985 THE ROLLS ROYCE
WOULD:

* COST $3.00
* GET 3 MILLION MILES PER GALLON,
* FIT 6 ACROSS THE HEAD OF A PIN, AND . . .
* DEVELOP THE SAME HORSEPOWER AS THE
  QUEEN MARY.

GIVEN ENOUGH TIME, MEMORY,
AND DISK SPACE . . .   ANYTHING IS
POSSIBLE.

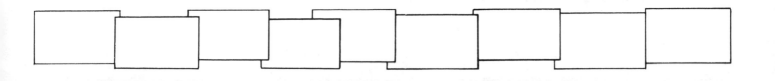

ANSWERS PRICE LIST

Answers .... 75 ¢

Answers (Requiring Thought) 1.25

Answers (Correct) 2.50

Dumb Looks Are Still Free

```
*********************************************************
```

A COMPUTER CAN MAKE MORE
ERRORS IN 2 SECONDS THAN 50
EXPERTS CAN IN 20 YEARS

```
*********************************************************
```

```
*********************************************************
```

IF BUILDERS BUILT BUILDINGS THE WAY
PROGRAMMERS BUILD PROGRAMS, THE
FIRST WOODPECKER WOULD HAVE
DESTROYED CIVILIZATION.

```
*********************************************************
```

CORPORATE STRUCTURE

CHAIRMAN OF THE BOARD
Leaps tall buildings in a single bound
Is more powerful than a locomotive
Is faster than a speeding bullet
Walks on water
Talks with God

PRESIDENT
Leaps short buildings with a running start and favorable winds
Is almost as powerful as a switch engine
Is faster than a speeding BB
Walks on water in an indoor swimming pool
Talks with God if special request is approved

VICE-PRESIDENT
Barely clears a quonset hut
Loses tug-of-war with a locomotive
Can fire a speeding bullet
Swims well
Is occasionally addressed by God

GENERAL MANAGER
Makes high marks on the wall when trying to leap buildings
Is run over by locomotive
Can sometimes handle a gun without inflicting self-injury
Dog paddles
Talks to animals

MANAGER
Runs into buildings
Recognizes locomotive two out of three times
Is not issued ammunition
Can't stay afloat with a life preserver
Talks to walls

TRAINEE
Falls over doorsteps when trying to enter buildings
Says "Look at the choo-choo"
Wets himself with a water pistol
Plays in mud puddles
Mumbles to himself

SECRETARY
Lifts buildings and walks under them
Kicks locomotives off the tracks
Catches speeding bullets in her teeth . . . and eats them
Freezes water with a single glance

She IS God!

HOW DID THEY EVER GET A PERMIT TO BUILD THE WORLD?

IF YOU LOVE SOMETHING,
   LET IT GO.
IF IT DOESN'T COME BACK,
   GO HUNT IT DOWN AND KILL IT.

HAPPINESS IS COMING!

ESCHEW OBFUSCATION

- BEER -

IT'S NOT JUST FOR BREAKFAST ANYMORE!

PLEASE DON'T TELL MY MOMMY I WORK _____. SHE STILL THINKS I'M A PIANO PLAYER IN A WHOREHOUSE!

IT TAKES A LOT LESS TIME TO DO IT RIGHT THE FIRST TIME THAN TO EXPLAIN WHY YOU DIDN'T!!!

GLOSSARY OF SALES AND BUSINESS TERMS

ADVANCED DESIGN — Beyond the comprehension of our sales force.

ALL NEW — Parts not interchangeable with existing models.

AUTOMATIC — You can not repair it yourself.

BREAKTHROUGH — We finally figured out how to sell it.

COORDINATOR — The person who sits between two expeditors.

DEVELOPED AFTER YEARS OF RESEARCH — Discovered accidentally.

ENERGY SAVING — When it's turned off.

EXPEDITE — To confound confusion with commotion.

FIELD TESTED — We don't have the equipment to test it at the factory.

FORWARDED FOR YOUR CONSIDERATION — You hold the bag for a while.

F.Y.I. — Found yesterday. Interested?

HERE AT LAST — We finally got it to work.

IMPROVED — Imported.

LIGHTWEIGHT — Falls apart.

RUGGED — Too heavy to lift.

WE WILL LOOK INTO IT — We hope you'll forget about it, too.

WE WILL ADVISE — If we figure it out, we'll let you know.

YOU NEVER KNOW HOW MANY FRIENDS YOU HAVE UNTIL YOU RENT A PLACE AT THE BEACH!

DEPARTMENT OF REDUNDANCY DEPARTMENT

NOTICE

To protect against losses due to hardware failures, this computer is equipped with a feature which automatically runs a program named "OREMA" (derived from the Latin *oremus*, for "*let us pray*") each 15 minutes. This program offers up selected prayers in the ancient languages of Latin, Hebrew, Arabic, and FORTRAN for the continued faultless operation of the CPU, disk drives, memory, and power supply.

At this time, no protection is offered for software bugs and errors, which are human faults, not hardware problems. However, a new version is being readied which will protect against these problems as well. It is to be called "SIN-OREMA".

NOTHING MOTIVATES A PERSON
MORE THAN TO SEE THE BOSS
PUTTING IN A FULL DAY'S WORK!

I refuse to have a battle of wits with an unarmed person.

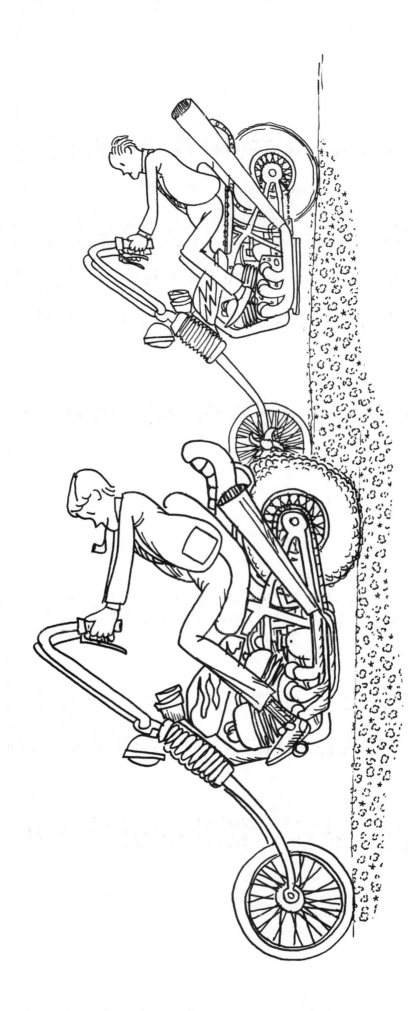

HELL'S LAWYERS

INTEROFFICE COMMUNICATION CODES

Management provides this list of communication codes to permit individuals freedom of expression and a more precise medium of communication between employees. More importantly, it will not impinge on customer relationships and others with senstive ears within hearing distance.

To preclude mistaking the communication codes for department or telephone numbers, Management has assigned them 800 or 900 series numbers to be used for your convenience.

800 Go piss up a rope.
801 Get off my back.
802 You've got to be kidding me.
803 Beats me.
804 What the hell.
805 It's so bad I can't believe it.
806 I hate this place.
807 This place stinks.
808 Lovely, simply lovely.
809 That damn clod.
810 Beautiful, just beautiful.
811 B.F.D.
812 Hang it in your ear.
813 I've got school tonight.
814 I don't give a damn.
815 Hot damn.
816 Bitchen.
817 Tell someone who gives a damn.
818 Don't get wise.
819 Do I care?
820 Pardon me, but you have obviously mistaken me for someone who gives a damn.
821 I didn't design the thing; I just maintain it.
822 It won't work.
823 Who called this meeting?
824 Fooled, and screwed beyond repair.
825 Eat it.
826 Your mother wears combat boots.
827 Stuff it in your shorts.
828 Don't get your pants in a bunch.

829 Just who do you think you are?

900 Cool it; this is my wife/husband.
901 Follow my lead.
902 I'm free this weekend.
903 Take your time; I don't want to be stuck with this ass for lunch.
904 Help me dump this mother.
905 I'm free tonight.
906 I'm tied up with my husband/wife tonight.
907 Call me at home to come back to work.
908 Call me back later; my wife/husband is here.
909 Let's take off sick together.
910 Meet you at the motel.
911 Let's snag them for tonight.
912 Let's do it in the dirt.
913 Let's eat.
914 Oh, what a nice lunch that would be.
915 You take the one on the right; I'll take the one on the left.
916 (Reverse of above)
917 Split, chickie/dude; don't hang around here when I have work to do.
918 People are beginning to talk.
919 Let's cool it for now.
920 I'd like to, but I can't handle it right now—maybe later.
921 Wasn't that nice?
922 Deep Throat.

SORRY!

   **I'VE ONLY GOT ONE OTHER SPEED,
   AND IT'S EVEN SLOWER!**

YOU'RE UGLY . . .

AND YOUR MOTHER DRESSES YOU FUNNY!

TIME SURE FLIES WHEN YOU'RE HAVING FUN!!!

LOOKING FOR SOMEONE
WITH A LITTLE AUTHORITY?

I've got as little as anybody!!

COWS MAY COME,

AND COWS MAY GO . . .

BUT THE **BULL** IN THIS PLACE

GOES ON FOREVER!

THIS JOB KEEPS CUTTING INTO MY DAY!

PROGRAMMERS DO IT ONE BYTE AT A TIME

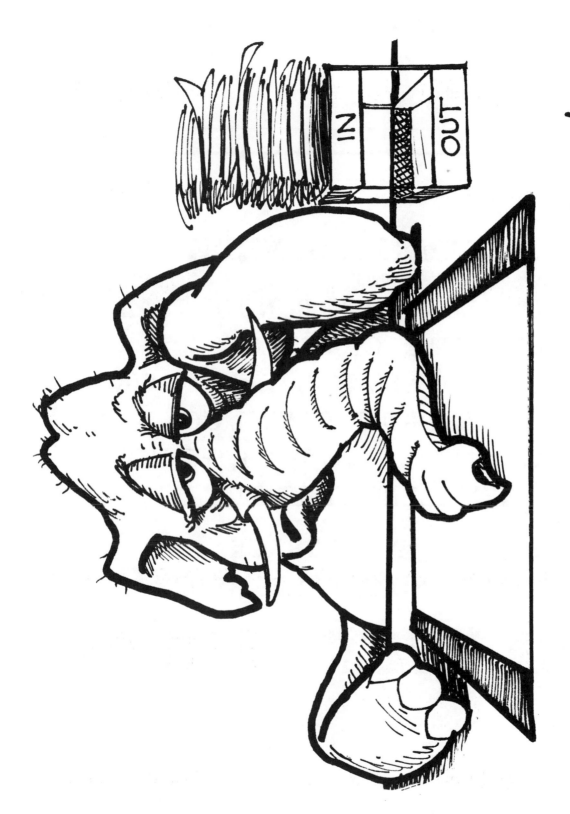

GOD, I LOVE THIS PLACE!

THE ENGINEER

I'M NOT ALLOWED TO RUN THE TRAIN;
  THE WHISTLE I CAN'T BLOW.
I'M NOT ALLOWED TO SAY WHICH WAY
  THE RAILROAD CARS WILL GO.
I'M NOT ALLOWED TO TOOT THE HORN,
  OR EVEN CLANG THE BELL;

BUT LET IT JUMP THE TRACK,
  AND SEE WHO CATCHES HELL!

TEMPUS FUGET
. . . . .et non combackabus!

ILLEGITEMI
NON
CARBORUNDUM

(Don't let the bastards get you down!)

THE OBJECTIVE OF ALL DEDICATED
COMPANY EMPOYEES SHOULD BE TO
ANALYZE ALL SITUATIONS THOROUGHLY,
ANTICIPATE ALL PROBLEMS, AND MOVE
SWIFTLY TO SOLVE THESE PROBLEMS WHEN
CALLED UPON.

. . . HOWEVER . . .

**WHEN YOU ARE UP TO YOUR ASS IN
ALLIGATORS, IT IS DIFFICULT TO
REMIND YOURSELF THAT YOUR
INITIAL OBJECTIVE WAS TO DRAIN
THE SWAMP!!**

DO NOT EMBARK ON VAST
UNDERTAKINGS WITH
HALF-VAST IDEAS

****

THIS IS NOT
A DRESS REHEARSAL...
THIS IS THE REAL THING!

The Salesperson

And in those days, behold, there came through the gates of the city a salesperson from afar off, and it came to pass as the day went by he sold plenty.

And in that city were they that were the order takers and they that spent their days in adding to the alibi sheets. Mightily were they astonished. They said one to the other, "How doth he getteth away with it?" And it came to pass that many were gathered in the back office and a soothsayer came among them. And he was one wise guy. And they spoke and questioned him saying, "How is it that this stranger accomplisheth the impossible?"

Whereupon the soothsayer made answer. "He of whom you speak is one hustler. He ariseth very early in the morning and goeth forth full of pep. He complaineth not, neither doth he know despair. He is arrayed in purple and fine linen, while ye go forth with pants unpressed.

"While ye gather here and say one to the other, 'Verily this is a terrible day to work', he is already abroad. And when the eleventh hour cometh, he needeth no alibis. He knoweth his line and they that would stave him off, they give him orders. Men say unto him 'nay' when he cometh in, yet when he goeth forth he hath their names on the line that is dotted.

"He taketh with him the two angels 'inspiration' and 'perspiration' and worketh to beat hell. Verily I say unto you, go and do likewise."

AUTHOR UNKNOWN

IF YOU CAN GET OTHERS TO
BELIEVE YOUR BALONEY,
YOU'LL BE VERY
SUCCESSFUL.
IF YOU BELIEVE
IT YOURSELF, YOU'LL BE
DEAD.

EXPERIENCE IS WHAT YOU GET WHEN
YOU DIDN'T GET WHAT YOU WANTED.

YEA,
THOUGH I WALK THRU THE VALLEY
OF THE SHADOW OF DEATH,
I WILL FEAR NO EVIL . . .
**FOR I AM THE
MEANEST S.O.B.
IN THE VALLEY!**

DON'T GO AWAY MAD . . .

JUST GO AWAY!

THIMK

WE NEVER MAKE MISTRAKES

PLAN AheAD

DON'T LET YOUR KARMA RUN OVER YOUR DOGMA!

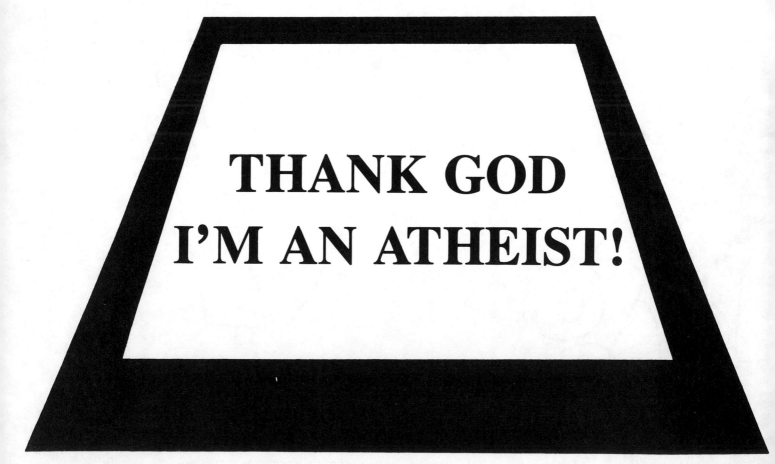

THANK GOD I'M AN ATHEIST!

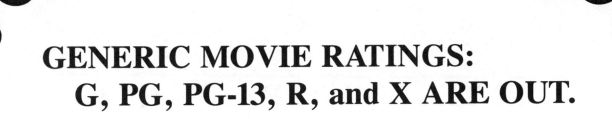

GENERIC MOVIE RATINGS:
G, PG, PG-13, R, and X ARE OUT.

WE NEED CONTENT RATINGS:

V - VIOLENCE
S - SEX
L - LANGUAGE
A - BAD ACTING
P - BAD PLOT
M - MONSTERS
(For parents of
small children!)

ENTER AT YOUR OWN RISK

"ALMOST"
ONLY COUNTS IN HORSESHOES
AND HANDGRENADES

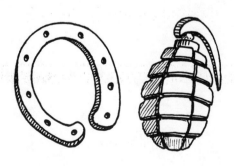

THE ENGINEER

During the French Revolution, a priest, a lawyer and an engineer were put on trial as enemies of the Revolution. The priest tried to defend himself by explaining how he had ministered to the poor, brought food to the hungry and tended the sick, but to no avail. He was sentenced to the guillotine. In those days, when a person felt he had been sentenced unjustly, he would demonstrate his feelings by making the supreme gesture — he would lie face-up rather than face-down in the guillotine. The priest did so. When the rope was tripped, it happened that the blade stuck in the channel about six inches above his neck. It was the rule that if ever the guillotine stuck, the victim was let free. So the priest was spared.

Then came the lawyer. He too argued for his life. He reminded them of the many criminals he had defended, of how he had served the poor without fee and had argued against unjust laws. But he too failed and was sentenced to die. And like the priest, he insisted on looking up at the blade as it descended. And in his case, too, the blade stuck in midair, and he was let free.

Then came the turn of the engineer. He pointed out that he had built the water works. There were public buildings and roads he had made for the people. He had never been engaged in politics, nor had he become rich at the people's expense. But these arguments fell on deaf ears. And he too expressed his contempt by lying on his back looking up at the blade. Then, just as the executioner was about to pull the rope, he let out a cry: "Look — I see your trouble. The rope has slipped off the pulley up there. No wonder the thing doesn't work."

AT THIS COMPANY,
SCIENCE ~~GOES DOWN ON~~
GETS DOWN TO BUSINESS!

AT THIS COMPANY,
WE ARE PUSHING BACK THE
~~FORESKIN~~ FOREFRONT OF SCIENCE!

IN THE SPIRIT OF...

... AND...

...WE SUGGEST

...AND...

"You can't soar with the eagles if you fly with the owls."

HOW CAN I SOAR WITH THE EAGLES WHEN I HAVE TO WORK WITH THE TURKEYS?

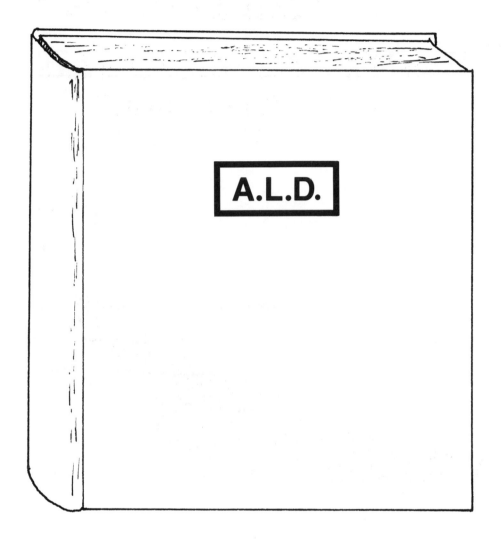

ACRONYM LOVERS'

DIGEST

SATISFACTION GUARANTEED

OR YOUR MONEY

TEARFULLY

REFUNDED

WE WELCOME ADVICE AND CRITICISM,

AND ALWAYS RUSH THEM

THRU THE PROPER CHANNELS.

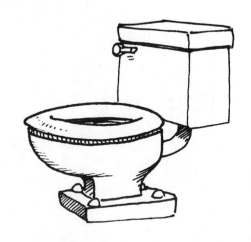

THE QUEEN
IS NOT GRANTING
AUDIENCES TODAY

THE KING
IS NOT GRANTING
AUDIENCES TODAY

AESOP'S REALISM

Once, there was a lion sitting on the edge of a great wood with a thorn in its paw. A little mouse chanced to be going by, and, seeing the lion's affliction, felt sorry for him. He went over to the lion, pulled the thorn out, and sat there smiling at the lion. The lion smiled back at him, and then, WHAM! ate him in a single gulp. The lion then carefully replaced the thorn, and sat back to wait for the next unsuspecting mouse.

COPIER STATIONERY

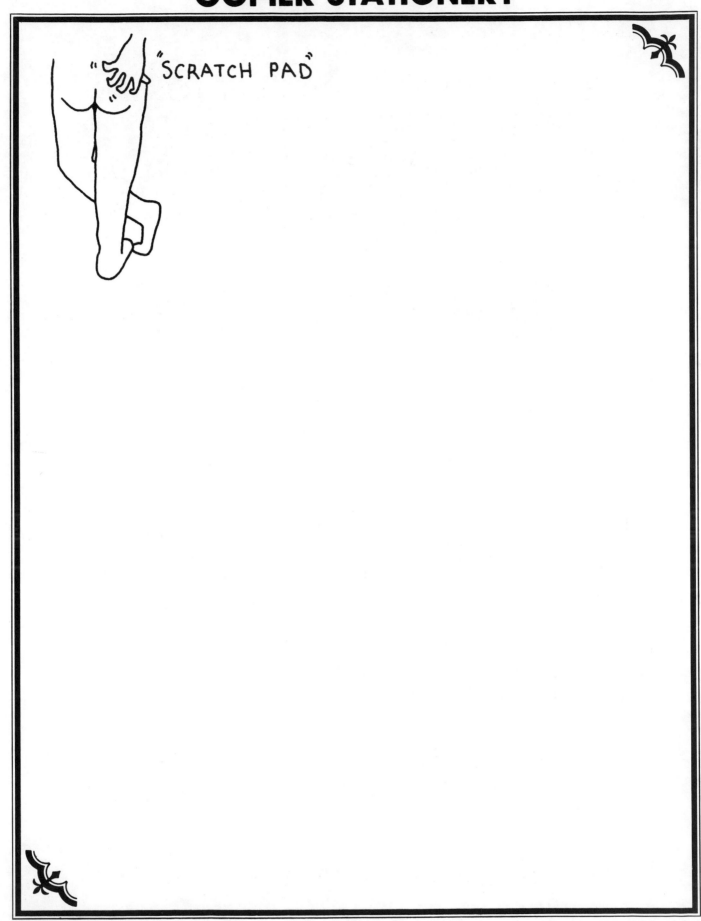

"SCRATCH PAD"

EXCUUUUUUUUUUSE ME, BUT . . .

YOUR COMPANY SEEMS TO HAVE "REDUNDANCY OF THE ACCOUNTS RECEIVABLES DEPARTMENT"!

(I ALREADY PAID THIS BILL!!!!)

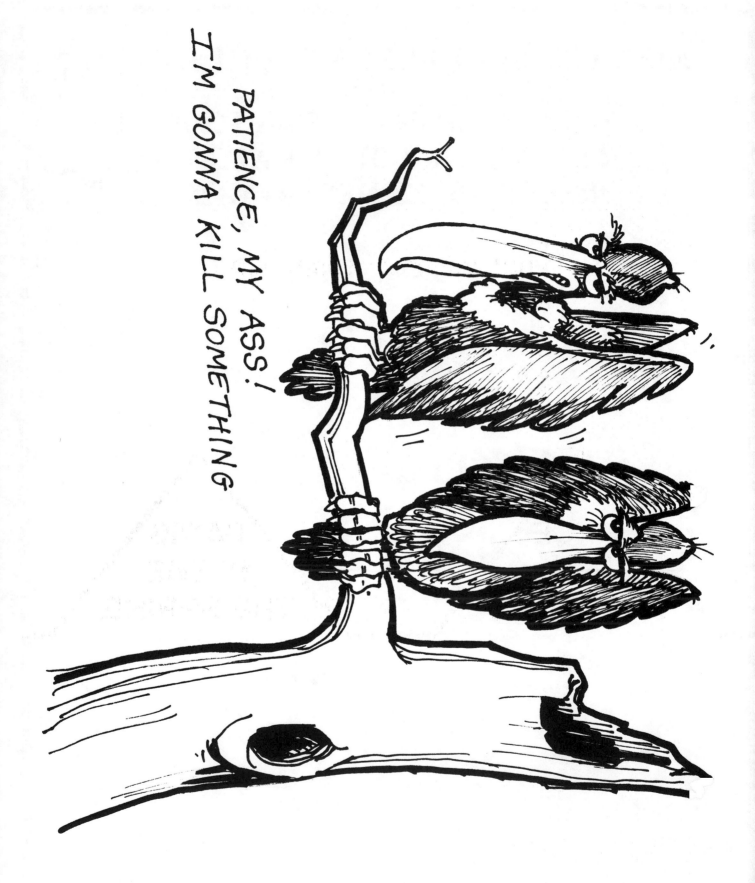

What do these really say?

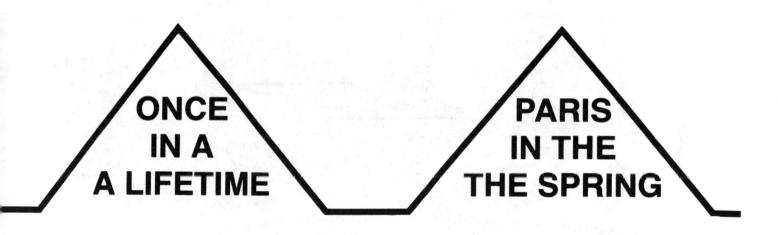

ONCE
IN A
A LIFETIME

PARIS
IN THE
THE SPRING

THE LAW OF LAST RESORTS:

THE ONE DAY YOU'D SELL YOUR SOUL, SOULS ARE A GLUT ON THE MARKET.

TELL PEOPLE THERE ARE 30 BILLION STARS,
  AND THEY'LL BELIEVE YOU.
TELL THEM THERE'S WET PAINT ON THE CHAIR,
  AND THEY'LL FEEL IT TO SEE.

THE SECRET OF SUCCESS IS SINCERITY . . .

ONCE YOU CAN FAKE THAT,
YOU'VE GOT IT KNOCKED!

NO JOB IS DONE
UNTIL THE PAPER WORK
IS FINISHED!

INSANITY IS HEREDITARY . . .
YOU GET IT FROM YOUR KIDS!

THE RATRACE IS OVER!
THE RATS WON!

Smithinski & Wessonovitch
POLISH DUELLING PISTOL

IT'S NOT WHETHER YOU WIN OR LOSE —
IT'S HOW YOU LOOK PLAYING THE GAME.

Lower Thy Voice, Lest
The Whole World Hear

EXPOSE YOURSELF TO COMPUTING

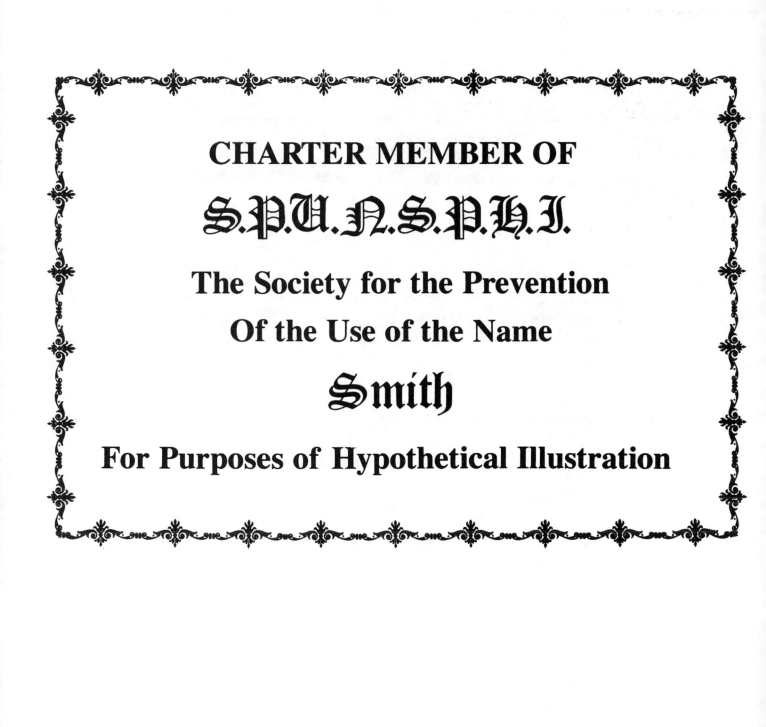

CHARTER MEMBER OF

𝕾.𝕻.𝖀.𝕹.𝕾.𝕻.𝕳.𝕴.

The Society for the Prevention
Of the Use of the Name

𝕾𝔪𝔦𝔱𝔥

For Purposes of Hypothetical Illustration

ARE YOU SAD BECAUSE NO ONE EVER CALLS YOU? WELL, CHEER UP!
I WROTE YOUR PHONE NUMBER IN 34 PUBLIC RESTROOMS YESTERDAY!

 ATTENTION!

THIS CAR IS HEADED FOR A SKI SLOPE.
CHAINS ARE REQUIRED.

(WHIPS, HOWEVER, ARE OPTIONAL.)

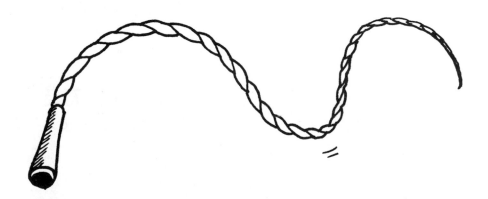

AS ENGINEERING
DESIGNED IT

AS MANUFACTURING
BUILT IT

AS FIELD SERVICE
INSTALLED IT

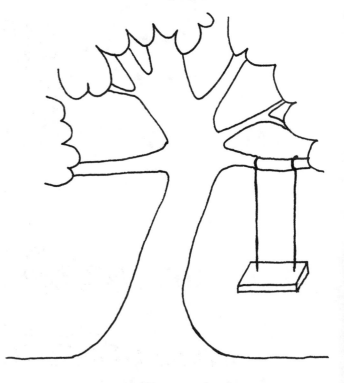

WHAT THE CUSTOMER
REALLY WANTED

A BATHROOM WITHOUT A LIBRARY IS LIKE
A LIBRARY WITHOUT A BATHROOM.

**YOU DON'T HAVE TO BE CRAZY
TO WORK HERE . . .
BUT IT SURE HELPS!**

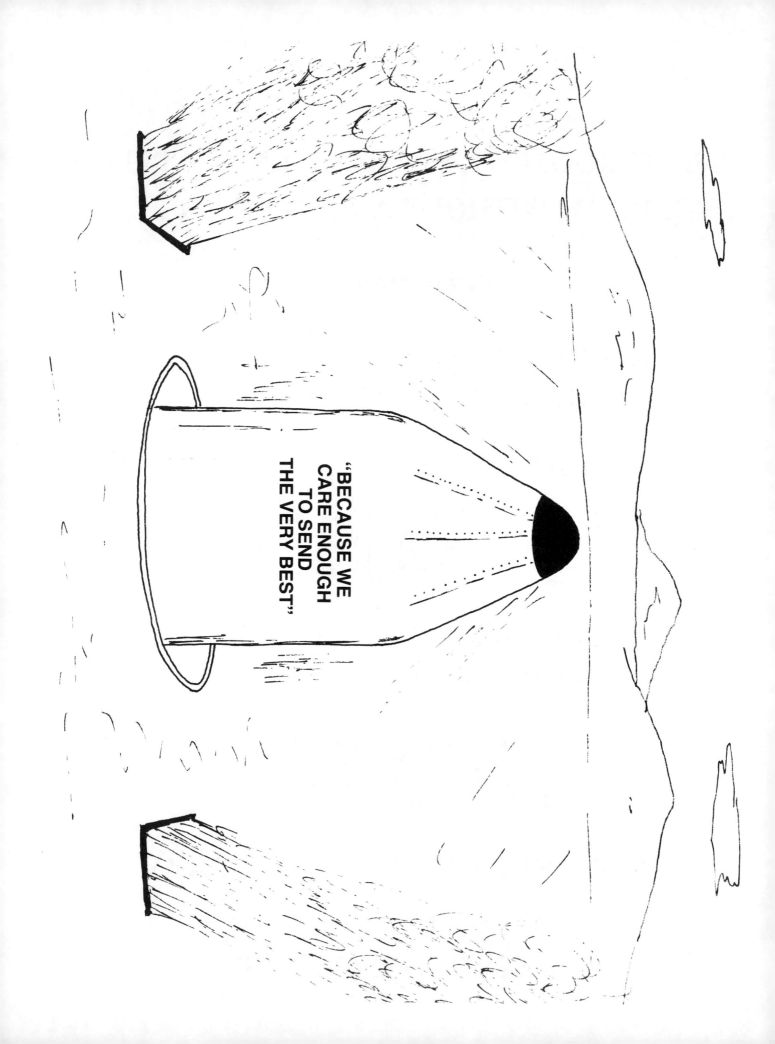

NOTICE

THIS DEPARTMENT REQUIRES NO PHYSICAL FITNESS PROGRAM:

EVERYONE GETS ENOUGH EXERCISE

JUMPING TO CONCLUSIONS,
FLYING OFF THE HANDLE,
RUNNING DOWN THE BOSS,
KNIFING FRIENDS IN THE BACK,
DODGING RESPONSIBILITY, AND
PUSHING THEIR LUCK.

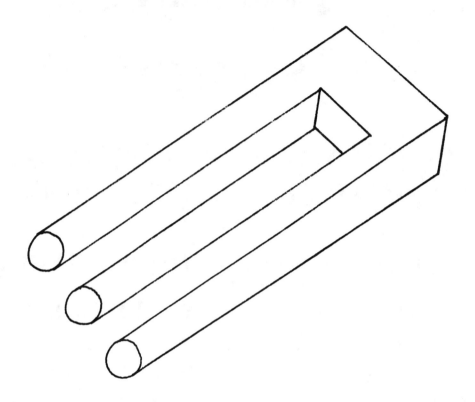

THE AIR FORCE'S
SECRET WEAPON
REVEALED!

COMPLAINT FORM

Please write your complaint in the handy space provided below. Be sure to print legibly.

☐

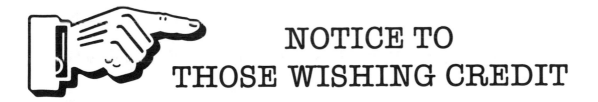

NOTICE TO
THOSE WISHING CREDIT

Our credit manager is Ms. Helen Boyle. All those desiring to arrange credit terms should go to Helen Boyle.

SEVEN STEPS IN A PROJECT

1. UNBRIDLED ENTHUSIASM — The new guy sees the projected performance specs, and reads in Aviation Week about all the wonderful things the airplane will be able to do.

2. CAUTIOUS OPTIMISM — The guy begins reading the original test reports, and realizes the specs will be awfully hard to meet.

3. QUIET DESPERATION — Interviews with the design engineers show that everything is behind schedule and over budget, and not one spec has a prayer of being met.

4. FRANTIC EFFORT — The guy works 80 hour weeks, for no extra pay, makes things work and fit that can't and won't; the test engineers bullshit the missing data from the tests that are never run.

5. THE SEARCH FOR THE GUILTY — The customer begins a purge of those responsible for the cost and schedule overruns. The guys who promised the impossible in the first place tell him to start looking at the workers.

6. THE PERSECUTION OF THE INNOCENT — All the guys who worked overtime for the last 18 months are laid off.

7. THE REWARDS TO THE NONPARTICIPANTS — The customer presents an award to the know-nothing management staff for delivery of an aircraft which, although late and over budget, performs better than specs and never breaks down.

IF YOU DON'T BELIEVE

THE DEAD COME BACK TO LIFE . . .

YOU SHOULD BE AROUND THIS PLACE

AT QUITTING TIME!

A STONE IS BREAD TO A STONEATER

**IT IS EASIER
TO GET FORGIVENESS
...THAN PERMISSION**

If we are closed, just shove
your money under the door.

****

WE, THE UNDERPAID, LED BY THE UNINSPIRING, INTO THE UNCHARTED, ASSISTED BY THE UNQUALIFIED, HAVE BEEN DOING THE IMPOSSIBLE WITH THE INADEQUATE FOR SO LONG, THAT WE CAN NOW DO ANYTHING, FOR ANYBODY, WITH NOTHING!

****

LONESOME?

Like to meet new people?

Like a change?

Like excitement?

Like a new job?

JUST SCREW UP ONE MORE TIME!!!

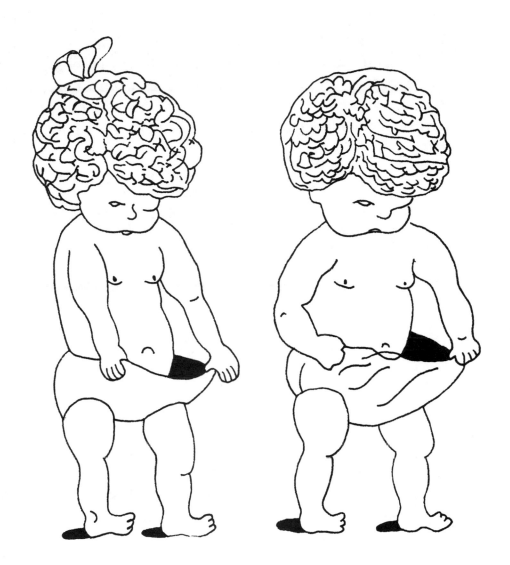

OH, THAT EXPLAINS
THE DIFFERENCE
IN OUR SALARIES!

TIME CHECK

An airline pilot called into Los Angeles Air Route Traffic Control Center (LA-ARTCC) requesting a time check, a fairly normal procedure. However, in the standard call-in, the name of the carrier was garbled. The controller answered, "I couldn't hear your company, Sir, but if you're from Laker, the time is two-four-zero-zero Zulu, if you're from Braniff the time is one-seven-zero-zero Local, and if you're from Golden West, the big hand is on the twelve and the little hand is on the five. Over."

---

2 × 2

Several scientists and technical types at a cocktail party were asked the simple question, "What is two times two?" The biologist quickly answered, "Oh, that's easy! Three!"

The engineer just smiled, pulled out his pocket calculator with ninety-two functions, pushed a few buttons, and announced, "Nope! It's 3.99999999999742."

The physicist sat down with a piece of paper and a pencil, and, after a few minutes, said, "Well, if you expand it using Taylor's Series, make a few simplifying assumptions, and disregard terms of order higher than two, you get . . . let's see . . . 3.75!" He smiled broadly.

But the mathematician, who had remained silent all along, answered last. "I don't know what the answer is," he said, "but I can tell you it's both unique and sufficient as a solution!"

**"OH, NOTHING MUCH --
JUST A LITTLE TALK WITH THE BOSS!"**

IMMEDIATE SERVICE
WHILE U WAIT

AND WAIT
AND WAIT
AND WAIT
AND WAIT
AND WAIT
AND WAIT
AND WAIT
AND WAIT
AND WAIT
AND WAIT
AND WAIT
AND WAIT
AND WAIT

 # NOTICE

The coffee machine is out of order today. Upon request, all employees who will be seriously affected by this situation will be started with jumper cables.

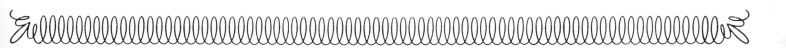

TRY OUR COFFEE.
NOBODY LIKES A COWARD!

BECAUSE I'M THE MOMMY, THAT'S WHY!

BECAUSE I'M THE DADDY, THAT'S WHY!

HOW TO BE A SUCCESSFUL EXECUTIVE

1. STUDY TO LOOK TREMENDOUSLY IMPORTANT.

2. SPEAK WITH GREAT ASSURANCE - STICKING CLOSELY, HOWEVER, TO GENERALLY ACCEPTED FACTS.

3. AVOID ARGUMENTS, BUT IF CHALLENGED, FIRE AN IRRELEVANT QUESTION AT YOUR ANTAGONIST AND INTENTLY POLISH YOUR GLASSES WHILE HE TRIES TO ANSWER.

4. CONTRIVE TO MINGLE WITH IMPORTANT PEOPLE.

5. BEFORE TALKING WITH A MAN YOU WISH TO IMPRESS, FERRET OUT HIS REMEDIES FOR CURRENT PROBLEMS. THEN ADVOCATE THEM STAUNCHLY.

6. LISTEN WHILE OTHERS WRANGLE. PLUCK OUT A PLATITUDE AND DEFEND IT RIGHTEOUSLY.

7. WHEN ASKED A QUESTION BY A SUBORDINATE, GIVE HIM A "HAVE YOU LOST YOUR MIND?" STARE UNTIL HE GLANCES DOWN, THEN PARAPHRASE THE QUESTION BACK TO HIM.

8. ACQUIRE A CAPABLE STOOGE, BUT KEEP HIM IN THE BACKGROUND.

9. IN OFFERING TO PERFORM A SERVICE, IMPLY YOUR COMPLETE FAMILIARITY WITH THE TASK - THEN GIVE IT TO THE STOOGE.

10. ARRANGE TO BE THE CLEARING HOUSE FOR ALL COMPLAINTS. IT ENCOURAGES THE THOUGHT THAT YOU ARE IN CONTROL AND ENABLES YOU TO KEEP THE STOOGE IN HIS PLACE.

11. NEVER ACKNOWLEDGE THANKS FOR YOUR ATTENTION - THIS WILL IMPLANT SUBCONSCIOUS OBLIGATION IN THE MIND OF YOUR VICTIM.

12. CARRY YOURSELF IN A GRAND MANNER. DISCOURAGE LIGHT CONVERSATION THAT MIGHT BRIDGE THE GAP BETWEEN BOSS AND WORKER.

13. WALK SWIFTLY FROM PLACE TO PLACE WHILE MUMBLING TO YOURSELF AS IF ENGROSSED IN AFFAIRS OF GREAT MOMENT. KEEP YOUR OFFICE DOOR CLOSED. GIVE ORDERS BY MEMORANDA. REMEMBER YOU ARE A BIG WHEEL AND YOU DON'T CARE WHO KNOWS IT.

14. PLAY BALL WITH THOSE WHO ACTUALLY DO YOUR WORK. GOLF WITH THE BRASS AND LOSE. DON'T PLAY WITH IN-PLANT SECRETARIES.

Would it upset you terribly if I asked
you to take your Silly-Ass problem
down the hall, per chance to find
someone who really gives a damn.

STACK OVERFLOW HURTS!

IT'S NOT A BUG . . .

IT'S A FEATURE!

WHEN YOU'VE SEEN ONE NUCLEAR WAR
YOU'VE SEEN THEM ALL

ARE WE HAVING FUN YET?

A WOMAN WITHOUT A MAN
IS LIKE A FISH
WITHOUT A BICYCLE.

—G. Steinem

Why is there so much month left at the end of the money??

OUR WORK HAS NUTRITIONAL VALUE.
IF YOU DON'T BUY IT, WE DON'T EAT!

WE DON'T GIVE A DAMN
HOW THEY DO IT IN L.A.!

 OEM IS MY MANTRA

I'VE GOT MNEMONIC PLAGUE!

HOW TO TELL A BUSINESSMAN FROM A BUSINESSWOMAN

He's agressive . . . . .She's pushy

He's good at details . . . . .She's picky

He loses his temper . . . . .She's bitchy
    (Because he's so involved with his job)

He's depressed . . . . .She's moody
    (So tiptoe past his office) . . . .(It must be her "time of the month")

He follows thru .She doesn't know when to quit

He's a man of the world .She's been "around"

He isn't afraid to say what he thinks . . . . .She's mouthy

He exercises authority . . . . .She's bossy

He climbed the ladder of success . . . . . .She "slept" her way to the top

If he is well dressed, he's fashionable . . . . .She's a clothes horse

He's confident . . . . .She's conceited

He drinks . . . . .She's a lush
    (because of excessive work pressure)

He's enthusiastic . . . . .She's emotional

THERE ARE ONLY TWO KINDS OF COFFEE . . .

WEAK -

the spoon stands up by itself;

STRONG -

the spoon dissolves.

FOR OUTSTANDING PERFORMANCE,

IS AWARDED

One Attaboy

One thousand "Attaboy's" qualifies the bearer to be a leader of men, work overtime with a smile, explain assorted problems to management, and be looked upon as a hero, with no raise in pay whatsoever.

NOTE: ONE "AWHELL" WIPES THE SLATE CLEAN, AND YOU HAVE TO START ALL OVER AGAIN.

"DON'T LOOK BACK...
   SOMETHING MAY BE GAINING ON YOU."

Satchell Paige

HOUSEWORK

ROTS THE MIND

WHEN IN TROUBLE
AND IN DOUBT
RUN IN CIRCLES
SCREAM AND SHOUT

ONWARD THROUGH THE FOG.

LIFE IS TOO SHORT TO DRINK BAD WINE

WHY, THAT'S FUNNIER THAN
WATCHING A PHYSICIST TIE HIS SHOE!

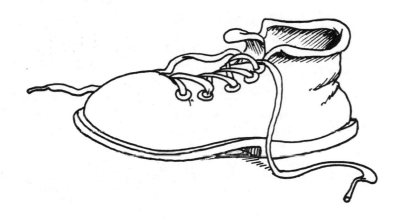

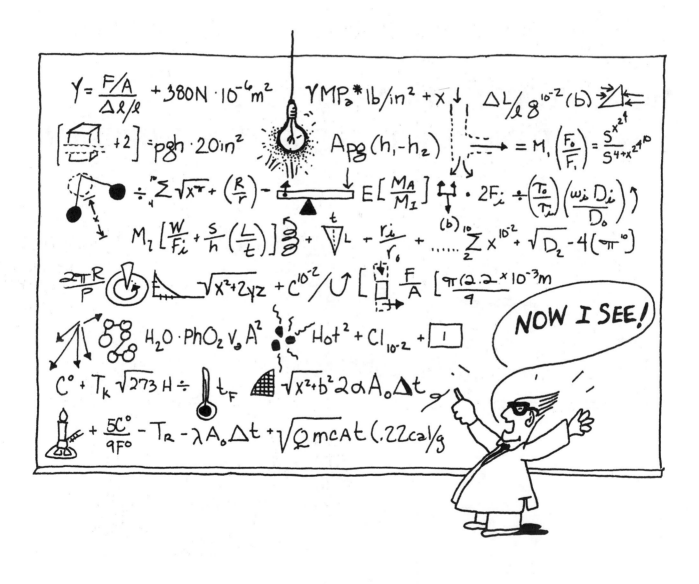

Fill in the blank

DO NOT

BOTHER,
BEWILDER,
TEASE,
CAJOLE,
ANNOY,
ENRAGE,
ANGER,
TEMPT,
FEED,
ENTICE, or
BULLYRAG . . .
THE
_____

A man who walks in another's tracks leaves no footprints.

I MAY BE GETTING OLDER,
BUT I REFUSE TO GROW UP!

MY GRANDCHILDREN
ARE SMARTER THAN
YOUR GRANDCHILDREN

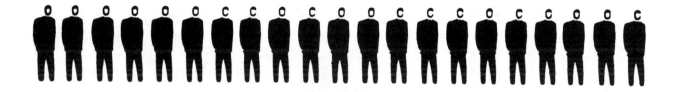

**Humans are the most complex
and wonderful things
they've ever seen.**

Once, long before the voyage of Columbus, there was an Indian tribe living on the eastern shores of the North American continent.

Presiding over the affairs of the tribe was a great chief, who had three squaws. The chief was a great warrior and statesman, known far and wide, and had established a custom whereby, at ceremonial feasts, he ate first, after which his sons ate; then came the other men and boys of the tribe, and lastly the women and girls — alas, not an uncommon type of custom in many early societies. However, as is also the custom in all societies, there are exceptions. The chief's youngest squaw was his favorite, and although she had borne him no sons, like the other two had, she was often the recipient of special privileges.

One day, a longboat arrived on the shore which had come all the way from the Gambia River of Africa — with an interpreter, no less — bearing explorers from that faroff land. The explorers brought gifts, including a prized hippopotamus hide for the chief. At an official welcoming feast, the delighted explorers presented the great chief with many hides, including the hippopotamus hide. The chief then gave the hides to his squaws to sit on during the ceremonies. Naturally, his favorite squaw sat on the hippopotamus hide.

After the chief ate his fill, he bade the explorers to eat with his sons — a great honor, indeed! As they began to eat, one of the explorers noticed that the chief had quietly given a plate of food to his favorite squaw, and that she was eating along with the men and boys. Noting this with interest, he inquired of the interpreter why such an incongruous event was occurring. The interpreter replied, "The chief thinks that the squaw on the hippopotamus is equal to the sons of the squaws on the other two hides!"

$$a^2 + b^2 = c^2$$

TABLE 4B:

FAA-APPROVED EMERGENCY CHECKLIST FOR A NIGHT-TIME FORCED LANDING IN A HELICOPTER (TOTAL POWER LOSS)

1. IMMEDIATELY LOWER THE COLLECTIVE PITCH CONTROL.

2. TWIST THROTTLE GRIP TO "ZERO" POWER POSITION.

3. EASE CYCLIC PITCH CONTROL FORWARD TO ACHIEVE A GLIDE SPEED OF 65 KNOTS.

4. DISABLE AUTO-IGNITE SWITCH.

5. SET FUEL-CONDITION SWITCH OFF.

6. MAINTAIN HEADING WITH PEDALS.

7. TURN ON LANDING LIGHT AT 100 FEET TO INSPECT LANDING AREA.

8. IF YOU DON'T LIKE WHAT YOU SEE, JUST TURN IT OFF!!!

NO MAN IS EVER GREATER OR MORE NOBLE
THAN WHEN HE FILLS OUT HIS RESUME.

AGE AND TREACHERY ALWAYS
OVERCOME YOUTH AND SKILL

BLESSED ARE THEY
WHO GO AROUND IN CIRCLES,
FOR THEY SHALL BE KNOWN
AS BIG WHEELS

ONWARD TO SQUARE B.

UNUSUAL CHEMICAL COMPOUNDS

MERCEDES BENZENE

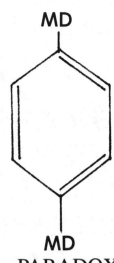

PARADOX

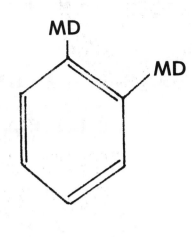

ORTHODOX

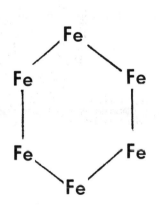

A FERROUS WHEEL

NO . . . IN ANY POSITION

METHYL ETHYL BATHROOM TILE

AN OXYGEN TENT

NOTICE

THIS IS A DARKROOM.
PLEASE KEEP THE DOOR
CLOSED.
IF YOU DON'T, ALL THE DARK
LEAKS OUT.

WHEN GOD MADE MAN
SHE WAS ONLY KIDDING

THE FIRST GREAT COMMANDMENT OF PARACHUTING

RESPECTETH THINE ALTITUDE,
ELSE SHALL THE EARTH
RISE UP AND SMITE THEE

YOU KNOW YOU'RE GETTING OLD WHEN . . .

—Everything hurts and what doesn't hurt, doesn't work.

—Your little black book contains only names ending in M.D.

—You get winded playing chess.

—Your children begin to look middle-aged.

—You finally reach the top of the ladder and it's leaning against the wrong wall.

—You're still chasing women, but can't remember why.

—You turn out the light for economic rather than romantic reasons.

—You sit in a rocking chair and can't make it go.

—Your knees buckle and your belt won't.

—You're 17 around the neck, 42 around the waist, and 96 around the golf course.

—Your back goes out more than you do.

—The little gray haired lady you helped across the street is your wife.

—Dialing long distance wears you out.

—A fortune teller offers to read your face.

—You get exercise acting as pallbearer for your friends who exercised.

—You sink your teeth into a steak and they stay there.

AFTER ALL IS SAID AND DONE,

A LOT MORE IS SAID THAN DONE

. . . SOUNDS LIKE

B.S. TO ME.

TO: ALL EMPLOYEES

FROM: THE MANAGEMENT

SUBJECT: EXCESSIVE ABSENCES

Due to the excessive number of absences from this establishment
the following rules and procedures will be put into effect as of
this date.

SICKNESS: No excuse. We will no longer accept your doctor's
statement as proof, as we believe that if you are able to go to
the doctor you are able to come to work.

DEATH: (OTHER THAN YOUR OWN), this is no excuse. There is
nothing you can do for them, and we are sure that someone else
with lesser position can attend to the arrangements. However, if
the funeral can be held in the late afternoon, we will be glad to
let you off one hour early, provided that your share of the work
is ahead enough to keep the job going in your absence.

LEAVE OF ABSENCE: (FOR AN OPERATION). We are no longer allowing
this practice. We wish to discourage any thoughts that you need
an operation as we believe as long as you are an employee here,
you will need all of whatever you have and you should not consider
having anything removed. We hired you as you are and to have
anything removed would certainly make you less than was bargained
for.

DEATH: (YOUR OWN). This will be accepted as an excuse; but we
would like a two week notice, as we feel it is your duty to teach
someone else your job.

Also entirely too much time is being spent in the restroom. In
the future we will follow the practice of going in alphabetical
order. For instance, those whose names begin with "A" will go
from 8:15 to 8:30, "B" will go from 8:30 to 8:45 and so on. If
you are unable to go at your appointed time, it will be necessary
to wait until the next day when your turn comes again.

A Martyr is someone
Married to a Saint

A CLOSED MOUTH
CATCHES NO FEET

WATCH YOUR LANGUAGE...
Here come some engineers!

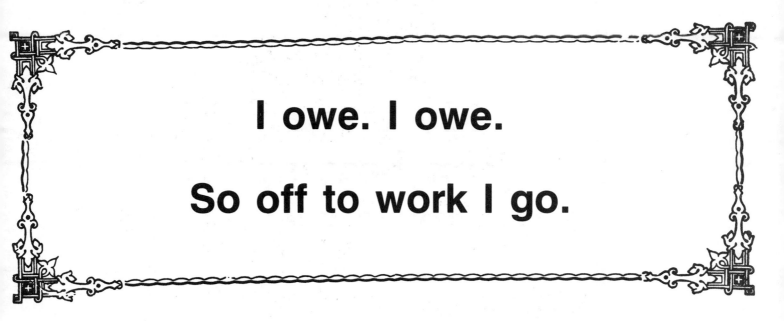

I owe. I owe.

So off to work I go.

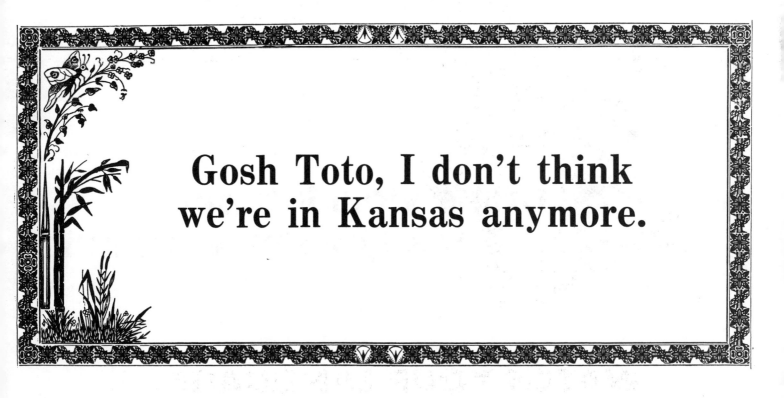

Gosh Toto, I don't think we're in Kansas anymore.

My lawyer
can beat up
your lawyer.

Crime wouldn't pay
If the government ran it!

FLOW DIAGRAM FOR GETTING OFF TO WORK

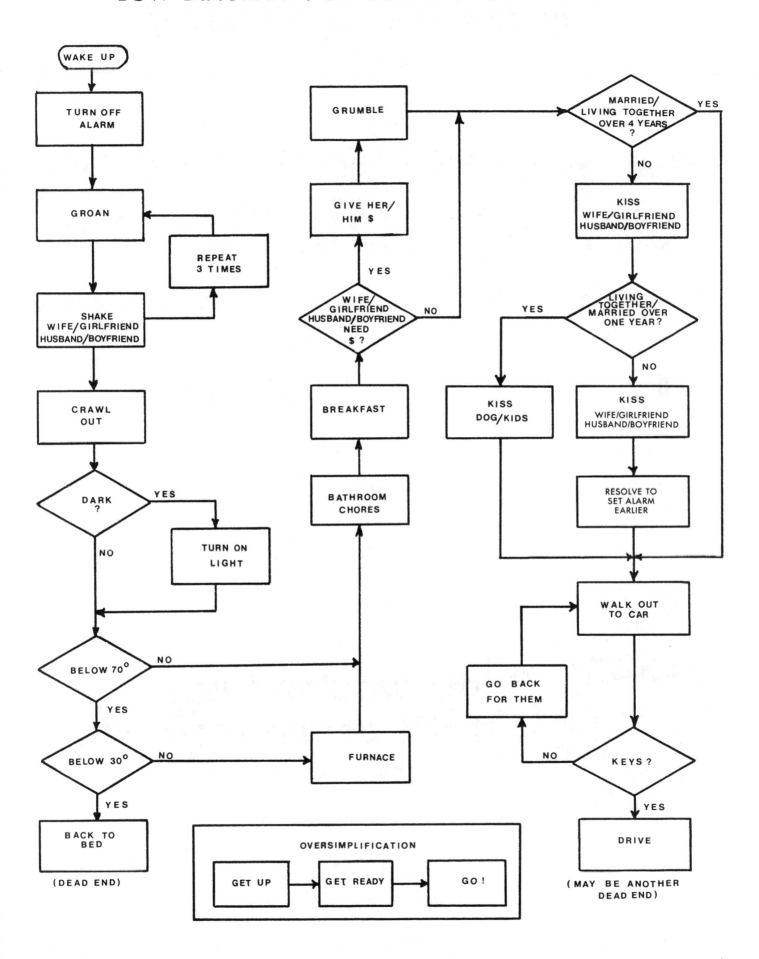

DON'T SQUEEZE THE SOFTWARE

DON'T BOTHER ME, I'M LIVING HAPPILY EVER AFTER

HIGH SCHOOL STUDENTS!
BE SURE YOU KNOW YOUR
TERMINOLOGY FOR 1986!

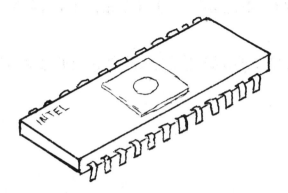

The Senior Prom

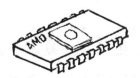

The Junior Prom

**FOR THOSE OF YOU WHO DON'T DANCE, PROM
STANDS FOR PROGRAMMABLE READ-ONLY MEMORY**

"It'll be a great day when schools get all the money they need, and the Air Force has to hold a bake sale to buy a bomber."

BE SURE TO ATTEND THE BUILD - A - B-1B - BOMBER BAKE SALE

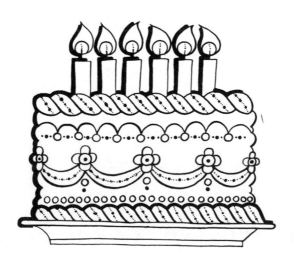

LABOR CHARGES:

IF YOU LEAVE YOUR STUFF AND GO AWAY:

$ _____ /hr.   (THE USUAL RATE)

IF YOU STAY AND WATCH:

$ _____ /hr.   (5 TIMES THE USUAL RATE)

IF YOU HELP:

$ _____ /hr.   (10 TIMES THE USUAL RATE!)

KWITCHERBELLYACHIN'

Avenge yourself...
live long enough to be a
problem to your kids!

If at first you don't succeed... you're about average.

DON'T STEAL...
(The government hates competition.)

ACHTUNG ALLES LOOKENPEEPERS

Das Komputenmaschine ist nicht für Gefingerpöken bei das rubbernecken Amateursen. Ist machen Spitzensparken mit Blowenfusen, Poppenkorken, und Schnappen der Springwerken. Alles Sightseeren keepen die Hands in den Pockets, Relaxen, und watchen die Blinkenlights!

VIRTUAL IS ITS OWN REWARD

FLOPPY NOW,
HARD LATER

I AM A MOTHER AGAINST DRUNK DRIVERS.
YOU JUST DRINK AND DRIVE
AND SEE WHAT A
MEAN MOTHER I AM!

A WOMAN'S PLACE
IS IN THE HOUSE
AND SENATE

YOU OVERFLOW MY STACK!

I/O EVERYBODY

~~~~~~

~~~~~~

MA BELL RUNS A BAUDY HOUSE

**DOING A GOOD JOB AROUND HERE IS
A LITTLE LIKE WETTING YOUR PANTS
IN A DARK SUIT . . .   YOU GET A WARM
FEELING, BUT NOBODY NOTICES.**

People who think
money isn't everything
don't know where to shop.

I finally got it all together
But I forgot where I put it!

The worst day fishing
is still better than
the best day working.

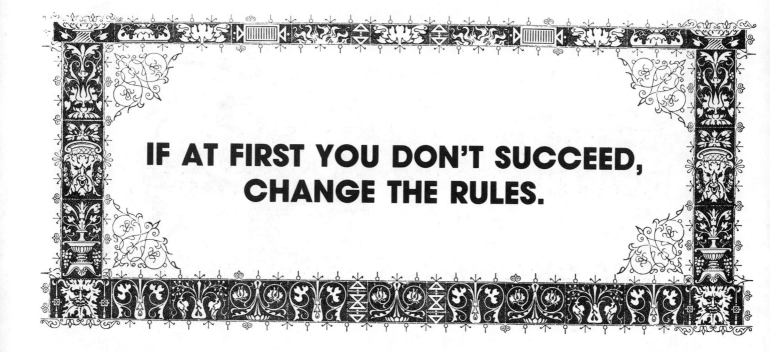

IF AT FIRST YOU DON'T SUCCEED, CHANGE THE RULES.

At Last!
Something that does the work of six men!
One Woman.

WHEN ALL ELSE FAILS, LOWER YOUR STANDARDS.

MURPHY'S LAW:

"IF ANYTHING CAN GO WRONG, IT WILL."

WHOEVER HAS THE MOST WHEN HE DIES WINS

MAKE SOMEONE HAPPY...

MIND YOUR OWN BUSINESS

YOUR HOUSE as seen by:

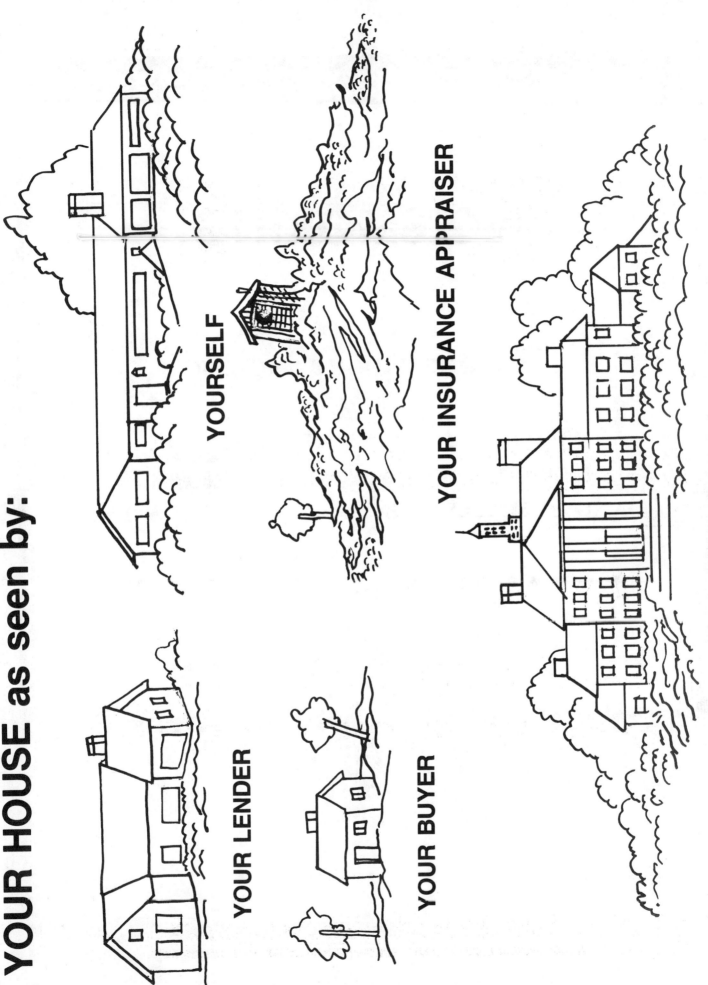

YOURSELF

YOUR INSURANCE APPRAISER

YOUR LENDER

YOUR BUYER

YOUR TAX ASSESSOR

NO SMOKING

ANYONE CAUGHT SMOKING

WILL BE HUNG BY THE TOENAILS

AND PUMMELLED INTO UNCONSCIOUSNESS

WITH AN ORGANICALLY-GROWN CARROT

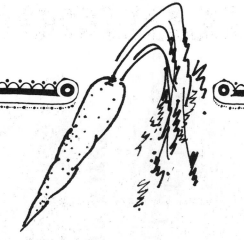

IF THE TRUTH BE KNOWN,
NO ONE WOULD BELIEVE IT ANYWAY!

IT'S NEVER TOO LATE
TO HAVE A HAPPY
CHILDHOOD

TOE TRUCK

KEEP SMILING . . .

the boss loves idiots.

Living Well is the best revenge!

APPLICATION TO JOINA DA MAFIA

Whatsa u name _____ U wage _____

Whatsa u howsa number _____ U streeta _____

Whatsa u bag? Hitta man ___ LONA ARRANGER ___ PROSITUTTA ___

Izza u a girl ___ or izza you a boy ___ (Justta checka wun, wiza guy!)

Iffa uzza girl, O BOY!

Putta down wearra u worka now _____

Wazza u ever inna de bigga howsa _____

Whatta for wazza u inna dere:

    I shoota wun guy _____ I keednappa sumbody _____

    Protecishun racket _____ Udda tingza _____

U wanna be a da bigga shotz sumdaze? YES ___ NO ___ EH! ___

U lika eata garlic? ___ PIZZA? ___ SALAMI? ___

U knowa how to maka de cement shooz? _____

U driva da car? _____ Whatsa da makke . . . .

    Cadillak _____ Buick _____ Linken _____

U lika Spaghetti _____ Calamari _____ Girlsa _____ Boysa _____

    (Justa pikka wun o I slappa you face!)

Hava u seena da Godfather? _____ or justa da movie? _____

Widda u antry u gonna gedda sumathingza u reely gonna likka . . . . .

1 pr. Darka Sunglazzes   1 lb. Mozzarella Cheesa

1 pr. Pointie Shooza   1 Whita Hat, widde Blaka Brim

1 pr. Cementa Shooza   1 Spumoni (Tutti-Frutti)

    (In case u fool arouna later!)

Wun blacka shirta widda whita tie

1 Kissa (Later, onna cheeka)

1 8x10 Picchur uffa Frank Sinatra

1 Happy Faca Button

Datza alla for now

        (Iffa u no likka it, I gonna giva

        u sumathinga myselfa, Wizzaguy)

Joinna da cluba now . . . . whila u still canna write.

        GIUSEPPI

        CUSTOMER RELASHUNS MANA

THE RULE OF EXPANDING HORIZONS:

IT WILL ALWAYS TAKE LONGER AND COST MORE THAN YOU THINK — EVEN IF YOU TAKE THIS RULE INTO ACCOUNT.

COLOR ME UNIMPRESSED

**If you don't know where to find me,
just listen for the sounds of battle!**

SUPPORT YOUR LOCAL BOOKIE

SURFING IS THE MOST FUN
YOU CAN HAVE
WITH YOUR SHORTS ON

TO MAKE A LONG STORY SHORT . . .

THERE'S NOTHING LIKE HAVING THE BOSS
WALK IN!

ARE YOU OFFERING A SOLUTION,

OR ARE YOU

JUST ANOTHER PART OF THE PROBLEM?

SOMETIMES THE DRAGON WINS

Create Your Own "Hang-Ups"!

ABOUT THE AUTHOR

Mr. Norris was born in New Jersey in 1947, into a world not of his own making. He shares a birthday, March 13, with Donald Duck, although he is 13 years the famous duck's junior. He moved to California with his family at age ten. Mr. Norris decided he wanted to be a physicist when he was six, after watching Walt Disney's "Our Friend the Atom" on television. Sixteen years later, after graduation from the University of California at Santa Barbara, he became — of all things — a physicist! He was laid off after three years of working with moon rocks and air pollution. (Periodic mass layoffs go with the turf in the Aerospace business!) For the next thirteen years he worked as a computer consultant, commercial diver, environmental analyst, charter pilot, gasohol entrepreneur and engineer. He is now back doing what he likes best . . . physics. A wide-ranging raconteur, known for his tendencies to join any kind of gab session at the drop of a hat, Mr. Norris is also known for his love of black humor and for putting funny signs all over his office at work.